ALONG *the* WAY

To Pastor Lloyd Greene —
I hope you enjoy the poems
and find a favorite or two —
David Tribby

DAVID C. TRIBBY

outskirts
press

The opinions expressed in this manuscript are solely the opinions of the author and do not represent the opinions or thoughts of the publisher. The author has represented and warranted full ownership and/or legal right to publish all the materials in this book.

Along The Way
All Rights Reserved.
Copyright © 2016 David C. Tribby
v3.0 r1.0

Cover Photo © 2016 thinkstockphotos.com. All rights reserved - used with permission.
Interior images courtesy Donna Whaley

This book may not be reproduced, transmitted, or stored in whole or in part by any means, including graphic, electronic, or mechanical without the express written consent of the publisher except in the case of brief quotations embodied in critical articles and reviews.

Outskirts Press, Inc.
http://www.outskirtspress.com

Paperback ISBN: 978-1-4787-7654-3
Hardback ISBN: 978-1-4787-7932-2

Library of Congress Control Number: 2016910899

Outskirts Press and the "OP" logo are trademarks belonging to Outskirts Press, Inc.

PRINTED IN THE UNITED STATES OF AMERICA

INTRODUCTION

Life is a journey, and along the way hope and faith have been nourished by the beauty found in nature, and in the lives of everyday saints.

Through every season's passing, I have found pleasure in walking. Mountain trails, country roads, even city streets have left indelible impressions. I remember more the longer walks, and have been glad when someone shared that time with me. A favorite dog has often been my willing companion.

Along the way, I have been spellbound viewing sunrises and sunsets, discovered the rich diversity of flora and fauna in quiet woodlands, breathed deeply upon mountain vistas, and paused to find peace by melodic waters. A love for nature is foundation to my writing, and like the varied adventures in walking, is better if shared.

Through a lifetime I have met many interesting people who have enriched my life experience. Sometimes the memory seems a composite, but there are people who stand out in their uniqueness. Several individuals were in *Gifts in Time* published in 2013, and others are found in this collection.

In *Along the Way* you will find an ageless child, a husband and parent, a veterinarian, and someone who feels blessed through a lifetime of countless gifts. From my cherished birthplace of Loudoun County Virginia, to family and working years spent in Augusta Georgia, and now a mountain home in western North Carolina, I am fortunate to have formed strong attachments and affection for the beauty in places where I have lived, and friendships with others who have shared a sense of belonging.

Two poems in this collection were first published in *The Reach of Song*, the annual anthology of the Georgia Poetry Society: "Walk Through the Orchard" in 2014, and "The Monument" in 2015.

ACKNOWLEDGEMENTS

My deep gratitude to Grace Bailey Heck for her suggestions, editing and encouragement. Her generosity of time and professional knowledge contributed greatly to the publishing of *Along the Way*.

I am also grateful to Donna Whaley for the artwork enhancing the section pages. Donna has a unique talent, and is recognized for her accomplishments in many art forms.

DEDICATION

With enduring affection, I dedicate *Along the Way* to my parents, John Derry Tribby and Margaret Graham Tribby, and cousin, Katherine "Bonnie" Graham Updegrove

CONTENTS

PROLOGUE 1

    LIFE JOURNEY 3

PART ONE 5

    CLIMBING TREES 7
    HOME TOWN 8
    GENESIS 10
    A SOLITARY CROW 11
    CATERPILLARS ARRIVE 12
    RECALLING INNOCENCE 13
    A ROCK'S JOURNEY 14
    RISE OF DAFFODILS 16
    BIRDS OF A FEATHER 17
    A WEB CONFINING 18
    AT RIVER'S EDGE 19
    DRAGONFLIES 20
    MORNING INTERLUDE 21
    HILLSIDE MEADOW 22
    CLOUD STRUMMING 23
    A GIFTED WHISTLER 24
    BEAUTY AND HOPE 25
    RAIN POOLS HERE AND THERE 26

MORNING GLORIES	27
PEELING AWAY BARK	28
A SPRING RAIN	29
HONEYSUCKLE	30

PART TWO   31

DOWN A COUNTRY ROAD	33
MY FATHER'S HATS	34
BOY SOPRANO	35
WITHIN THE POND	36
SHENANDOAH	37
WALLET OF A YOUNG MAN	38
LOUDOUN VALLEY	39
ROCK OF MYSTERIES	40
A DOG'S DEFENSE	42
A BIRD'S PLAINTIVE SONG	43
FRAGILE KITTEN	44
DRAFT HORSES	45
LIMERICK LADY	46
GARDEN SYMMETRY	47
STARTLING PHEASANT	48
OCTOBER SURPRISE	50
STONE FENCE	51
A VIOLIN'S VOICE	52
FELINE BEHAVIOR	53
AFTERNOON IN A GREEN FIELD	54
CARILLON IN BYRD PARK	56
THIS WATAUGA	57
HILL TOP HEALING	58

PART THREE 59

AN ORIOLE NEST	60
REHOBETH	62
REMEMBERING AN UNCLE	64
OLE MISERICK	65
FIRE CALL	66
JANNEY'S STORE	67
GENTLEMAN OF OUR TOWN	68
SYMPHONY IN THE BARN	70
SHORT HILL FIRE TOWER	71
IRIS AND DAYLILLIES	72
FINDING PATIENCE	74
GOLDEN MOMENTS	75
DAWN AT TYBEE PIER	76
NIGHT OF FULL MOON	78
ARTIST ON THE SQUARE	79
WALKING DONEGAL	81
OFF PARKWAY TRAIL	82
TO DOC WATSON	84
BEST FRIENDS	85
NEW CALENDAR	86
MOUNTAIN SPRING	88
DREAMS ESCAPING	89
FINDING AN OTTER	90
WANTING FOR LYRICS	91
FALLING LEAVES	92
SUMMERVILLE	93

PART FOUR   95

ANCHORING ROOTS	96
SELF DISCOVERY	97
FIRST SNOWFALL OF WINTER	98
LIGHTS THROUGH SNOW	99
EYES OF THE DEER	100
SUDDEN SUMMER STORM	101
HANDS WE HOLD	102
HIS CHAIR	103
QUESTIONS IN THE JOURNEY	104
IN PROFILE ONLY	105
WINDOWS ABOVE THE SNOW	106
THEIR PEW	107
IN SPRING'S WARMTH	108
NO CAGE AS LOVELY	109
YOUR FACE	110
WINTER WIND	111
THAMES WATCHING	112
WHITEOUT	113
DEAR FRIENDS	114
OBELISK	116
PREDICTABILITY	118
THE GIFTING TREE	119
LIFTING WIND	120
WALK THROUGH THE ORCHARD	121
DOG WALKS	122
FEARS IN THE DARK	123
PANSIES IN WINTER	124

YELLOW MAPLE	125
DACHAU JOURNEY	126
FALL OF A SILVER MAPLE	128
GARDEN DAWNING	129
SAYING GOOD-BY	130
HIGH WATER BRIDGE	131

PART FIVE   **133**

THE MONUMENT	135
AN EVENING WALK	136
THESE HANDS	138
A ROAD THROUGH MAPLES	139
AN INNER VOICE	140
A LEAF FALLS NEAR	141
HERE IN TIME	142
A LONELY AGING DAY	143
OUR NEIGHBORS WERE FRIENDS	144
RHYTHMS OF ROCKING	145
LEAVES THAT REMAIN	146
A WHISPER WOULD SUFFICE	147
DRAWN BY LIGHT	148
NEVER TO CATCH A BUTTERFLY	149
TENTATIVE PRESENCE	150
FLEETING MEMORY	151
BELLA	152
AGING THRESHERS	153
FALLEN WINDMILL	154
TOASTING THE YEARS	155
GRAY BEGINNING	156

AGING PETS	157
DISCOVERY AT CREEK'S EDGE	158
NEGLECTED TOO LONG	160
A RECLUSE STILL	161
HERE THEY REST	162
APPARITION	163
ELDERLY LADY WALKING	164
LOVE'S DISCOVERY	166
THE WALK OF MY LIFE	167
GIFTED BY GENES	168
EPILOGUE	**171**
THE CANDLE	173

PROLOGUE

LIFE JOURNEY

An intrepid traveler for much of his life,
unfolding days upon innocent beginnings,
evenings believing enough was done,
and thinking back with the feeling
it truly seemed at times as play.

The old man felt a sense of well being
effortlessly relaxed on time's winding,
comfortable within himself
having embraced life's adventures,
obstacles in his journey refreshing purpose,
better still, next steps becoming easier.

PART ONE

CLIMBING TREES

Through the years of my youth
I was a climber and sitter in trees.
Our sycamore gave generously
of limbs in stair-step nearness,
the maples nearly as good,
but denser foliage obstructed viewing.

At the highest point of the climb
I would look west to the town water tower,
and beyond to the Blue Ridge Mountains.
There were nearer interests as well
that seemed like spying at times,
and I didn't avoid that as a child,
it became part of the appeal.

Being up the tree had advantages,
a kind of hiding, being unreachable,
and some large limbs providing seating
while watching below and beyond.
I climbed without knowing fear,
although there were days with wind
when the tree would lean and sway,
and I would hug the strong, secure trunk.

Not until my own children
became climbers of trees
did I ever feel uneasy about climbing,
and then I, rather than they,
learned a fear of heights.

HOME TOWN

The town was surrounded by farms,
mostly dairy, but others thrived as well.
If you weren't a farmer, your grandparents were,
like the first family, Purcell, who lent their name,
and adding ville sounded better than burg,
the name resonating a legacy of a family gone.

There were no cemeteries within our town.
People still died, but most were buried in Hillsboro,
or the windy old churchyard near Bloomfield.
I asked why our town had no burial grounds
and was told, "people here are too busy with living."

The town fostered a spirited sense of belonging,
churches of most denominations,
fair grounds, skating rink, local baseball,
summers of annual 4H fairs and carnivals.
It was a proud and bustling farming-built town,
the business and cultural center of the Loudoun Valley,
and stores where people shopped while visiting.

State route seven became main street
connecting our lives to places east and west,
and conspicuously notable the middle of town
which was wanting of a full intersection,
a half block separating north and south streets,
those being paved over horse and buggy roads.

The Short Hill range northwest of town,
the mountains of the Blue Ridge beyond added
dimensions,
and looking there we found the day's weather.
I walked country roads and tree-lined streets
passing homes where no strangers lived,
and growing up felt safe and free, open to discovery.

There were two rules our parents had us live by:
stay out of fields with bulls and be home by dark.

GENESIS

Seeds of life scatter earthward
pirouetting from parent trees,
or soar on winds of chance
miles from parent wildflowers.

In fields and crevices numbers matter,
each tiny grain on a lonely journey
struggles to gain a foothold,
as hours and years go unmarked.

Rains come and open pathways,
and I sense seeds in mindless digging
reaching deeper before first frost,
warmth of the snowflakes blanket.

Seeds must know a sun to germinate,
and in broad and narrow spaces
against odds defying each one singly,
they twist in anguish and turn on hope.

Next year or decades hence,
green shoots will come one spring,
for seeds do not command predictions,
genesis waits until life happens.

A SOLITARY CROW

A solitary crow came for three winter days,
and I recall being told in my youth "beware of the crow."
Late one gray afternoon, I noticed him
standing on the border fence, staring directly at me,
head tilting and bobbing, mute on the sunless day.

The next day, he was back, topping a fence post,
and I thought how like a sentry standing there.
He nodded his head while watching me,
then fanning his wings, opened his beak,
pink tongue contrasting to all that black,
our staring mutual, then he turned and flew away.

The third day he came, brazenly approaching,
walking on the sitting porch, up and down he looked,
his eyes focused, body weaving, weight shifting foot to foot,
then spoke in a language I did not know.
I asked him to stay, words on which he seemed to lean,
staring back at me, before his wings sought the winter sky.

I have watched for him through three seasons passing,
wondering if he was entrusted with a gift,
speaking in tongues from someone lost to me,
far beyond the falling sun and rising moon,
bringing a message only crows can carry.

CATERPILLARS ARRIVE

I picked up a soft caterpillar
holding it with care, feeling it walk,
safely above hazards of travel
offering respite, a place to talk.

Finding them yesterday on our lawn,
they were here unseen before we knew
their colors so like the autumn hues,
easy to miss on a casual view.

Leaves of October blanket each path,
and I try to walk with care today
not to step on others passing through,
hoping that some will decide to stay.

This one I've chosen briefly to hold,
in woolly colors of black and brown,
its body squirming on tiny legs
protests being held, quickly wants down.

Its wish is to find shelter and food
for the promise of flight still survives,
not making woolly worm predictions...
how cold the nights when winter arrives.

RECALLING INNOCENCE

Occasions forgotten emerging from childhood,
images selectively imprinted, stored away,
retained until dreams bring them as lost gifts.

Glimpses of faces, some wanting names,
chasing a firefly's luminescence on a summer evening,
an early December snowfall found on dawn's arrival,
a first puppy's soft kisses, freely given,
all of these, and so much more long in waiting.

Some nights from sleep's depths harbored images arrive,
and I wonder where they hide in my waking hours.
Emerging to visit in the quiet hours after midnight
I reach to embrace them before they lose their way.

A ROCK'S JOURNEY

The rock was off the path a few steps,
easily missed in passing through.
I'm not sure why it caught my eye,
others much the same scattered around,
but it claimed ground alone, among tall ferns,
half covered with moss, by aging bound.

With little thought, pausing the day's walk,
then kneeling down where green ferns grow,
I carefully pried the moss away.
It wanted to stay in that sheltered place
requiring an effort more than I thought
to lift it up from its familiar space.

I stood up from my kneeling there,
taking the rock away from the ferns,
walked to the edge of the nearby creek
thinking to wash its surfaces clean,
or throwing it to the current's whims,
not by other walkers ever seen.

Considering choices of which to do,
not favoring one more than the other,
thinking that some things don't like change
want to be admired in their own way,
preferring to remain just as they are,
while this for me had simply been play.

Walking to where we had earlier met,
I knelt again in the sheltering ferns,
then placed it carefully to lie just so,
grooming the moss to cover the same,
so just the rock and I would know,
remember the choice to which we came.

RISE OF DAFFODILS

Bring on the daffodils, its spring!
Emerging predictably on the nearer sun,
yellows and greens rise above dormant grass,
and while uncertain are the moods of March
bringing hesitant steps to season's fullness,
winds of change will arrive in time.

I watch the buds on silent trees,
our dogwood long now in waiting,
thinking that arrival of daffodils
bridges hours before season's fullness,
prelude to pinks and whites of fruit trees,
and azaleas wearing magic again.

BIRDS OF A FEATHER

Defining imprinting must occur soon after birth,
cardinals prefer cardinals, and wrens pair,
and I've wondered is that just as true for us,
our initial comfort zone learned nest early.

Lately I've seen orioles and sparrows together
ground feeding beneath my seed feeders,
and although they don't seem to object
their flights away take different paths,
nesting choices programmed, made long ago.

For a time, I wondered how it happens,
this pairing up and traveling only with kind,
then one spring day of sensual fragrance
when birds were coupling on familiar calls,
a lone dove came, cooing a plaintive song.

A WEB CONFINING

A web confining, restricting,
draping with expectations,
and I walked under its shadow,
and that was true for others I knew.

Aspirations and dreams went knocking,
a fortuitous voice quietly speaking
about bridges that cross dark waters,
of scaling walling impediments.

Barriers met were preludes to accepting,
occasions to prove truth sufficient;
remaining undaunted in purpose
I found the web no match for faith.

AT RIVER'S EDGE

I sit beneath the river's willows,
resting and avoiding serious intent
caring little for the passage of time,
glad for the moment-by-moment intrusions.

I discover in the river's gentle current
swirls of feeding fish, stilted birds focusing,
while surrounded by a myriad of life forms,
winged and not, large and minuscule,
each one chasing calories within passing hours.

I watch turtles at water's edge, in sunny places,
not feeding, transfixed by deeper need,
patiently disengaged while their blood is warmed,
motionless as the smooth stones they rest upon.

The timelessness of the day rewards my senses,
and I inhale living fragrances rising off the water,
vapors of past and future at river's edge,
thinking on eternity in all the vibrancy of life.

DRAGONFLIES

I watch the busyness of dragonflies
skimming above the pond's silent face,
rising and darting on transparent wings,
intriguing, remarkable pilots of flight.

Their aerial acrobatics fascinate,
fearless in seemingly erratic flying,
charging out of the sheltering cattails
finding prey at the pond's gray surface.

One large dragonfly deftly maneuvers
to escape the sudden rise of a hungry bass,
in changing direction by quick reversing,
and the immediacy of instinct to survive.

MORNING INTERLUDE

In the interlude after dawn's first light,
I sense rhythms on the restless air
moving through the oak tree's webbing,
bringing a second awakening.

A pair of cardinals arrive to feed,
and I watch them dance in the tea olive,
then fly to my feeder, their eyes alert,
watching movements in morning's shadows.

I become captive to what I witness,
enchanted over the beauty before me,
observing simple bird skills, aeons old,
briefly altered by a feeding station
while feathers brighten on the rising sun.

HILLSIDE MEADOW

While I still breathe of summer's fragrance,
that essence of future life becoming,
lay me in the embrace of the hillside meadow
where sunbeams and wildflowers meet.

Place me at eye level with butterflies and honeybees
feeding on the abundance of clover and daisies,
and I will listen for the meadowlark's song.

When the day falls behind the blue mountains
come for me, I'll be waiting in patient repose.
If I breathe, cover me once again with your kindness,
or not, cover me with the warm earth at hand,
knowing that I sleep in contentment
beneath the beauty of an endless day.

CLOUD STRUMMING

A hillside of buttercups and clover
softly and lively the earth in season,
the sky overhead fracturing sun rays,
cloud shapes forming, fragmenting,
persuading us to join in the day's passing.

Favoring an abundant view above,
we rest in the fragrant yellow field
to surprise ourselves in what we find,
each asking what the other sees above,
attempting to solve the not so obvious.

Our fingers pointing up and waving
as we playfully strum the crowded sky,
finding, sharing discoveries, agreeing,
or differing in not seeing the same
within the broken sky's constant flux.

Upon the slanting of the falling sun
our clouds have claimed golden edges,
and we rise in that enchantment
holding onto breathless moments,
watching the sun sliding slowly west.

A GIFTED WHISTLER

In Memory of Melvin Ryon

He whistled up the farm's ground hogs
in the rolling pastures to the south,
and we watched them rise up from burrows,
alert, searching on the stranger's song.

A warbling whistler as we walked
and I was duly impressed by him,
older than me, but still young,
willing to have a hiking companion.

I knew how to whistle but not to his level,
two tones emanating in unison
like two flutes in synchronous play,
not unlike a yellow warbler in full voice.

Our summer walk through ripe meadow grass
reaching at last the border woods,
where we sat in the afternoon shade
while he whistled familiar bird calls.

I glimpsed bright flashes of color
in hiding places within the trees' foliage;
to my delight called up voices answered
in trusting mimicry the songs they knew.

BEAUTY AND HOPE

Watching wind move through maples, I know beauty,
the leaves' pale undersides weaving a brightness
within the darker green of summer's fullness,
moving in blending waves, turning far above
deeply anchored roots where their future begins.

There is bonding in eyes fixed on other eyes,
and I see the nursing mother's joy defined,
her infant busy suckling,
trusting, looking upward into hopeful eyes,
and I am gifted to behold the future.

Life's best moments can be lost blindly searching,
believing we are missing something beyond,
when in the nearest presence of sight and touch
hours of unmeasured worth are easily found,
where beauty and hope offer daily giving.

RAIN POOLS HERE AND THERE

Raindrops join their soft round edges
becoming pools the earth allows,
mirrors to brief passing showers
enhancing roses' sweet perfume.

I watch parting clouds float over June hills
somewhere to the east to linger again,
and I picture puddles on distant ground.

The air glistens upon sun's arrival,
two doves pausing to fan raindrops from wings,
then fly away to chase distant rainbows.

If roses and doves live where clouds have gone,
a visit would be nice on days like this.

MORNING GLORIES

The garden gate opens to discovery
in this hour when the sun slants gently,
glistening on the dew where it touches,
and my ritual of early arrival
to find the morning glories' vibrancy.

Mockingbirds and wrens ahead of me
drawn by sight and favored memories,
seeking this garden, its abundance of life,
the pleasure of living seen on their wings,
lyrics of their songs in joy of feeding.

My favorite sitting place is the turned earth
along the edges of the tallest corn,
upon which the vines entwine to climb high,
and within the partial sun reaching there
the morning glories' doors open widest.

The day's progression will find them wilting,
bees moving on to other flowers near,
but I think nothing so appealing as glories
daily renewing upon the sun's bright climbing,
until birds fly to shade in the maple tree.

PEELING AWAY BARK

We peeled bark from the gallant sycamore,
for no other reason than our pleasure,
breaking large pieces into smaller sizes,
folding to fracture, finding imagined designs,
busy hands innocent in simplest things.

It did not harm the tree, and looking up
I found a sublime whiteness in highest branches,
long silvery seductive limbs, wearing no bark,
appearing virginal and distant, etching the clouds,
hovering out of reach, framing the winter day.

A SPRING RAIN

Gray roofs below my sitting window
slanting in sameness, darker now,
accepting raindrops one by one,
releasing them in flowing sheets,
and I watch people come and go
dipping heads, moving quickly,
not escaping their roof's spilling.

I have nowhere that needs me now
feeling immune to hurrying about,
no desire to dodge the watery torrent
waiting outside my door.

I'll walk when the rain falls softly
when there will be no need to hurry,
dark clouds racing eastward,
time to step into puddles of spring,
look for a rainbow striping the sky.

HONEYSUCKLE

I will leave the honeysuckle untouched
neither thinning nor groom to chosen design,
but allow the growing as if owning will,
in wild profusion claiming its destiny,
the garden fence to carry that rambling.

Small birds will nest there, brown rabbits burrow near,
while honey bees thrive on ripe nectar,
then carry that lusty sweetness they imbibe
to hive-bound workers in woodlands secluded.

I will spend entranced hours watching butterflies dance
to settle now and again on yellow white blooms,
and marvel at this loveliest of life stages.
I will find reward in the hours after twilight,
when warm gentle breezes lift through open windows
honeysuckle fragrance into my sleeping room.

PART TWO

DOWN A COUNTRY ROAD

There are times like today when a walk is best
leading nowhere planned, even if it is circuitous;
decisions made on a moment's persuasion,
walking a country road where crossroads abound,
and wheat ripening in fields around.

Without effort, my senses lead the way,
or inspired instinct wills me in choosing.
In the natural seeding on roadway edges
I find jewels while pausing, closely observing
daisies, asters and milkweed, in splendid disarray,
waving gently on the languid summer breeze.

On another day while at a leisurely pace,
I found bees overwhelmed by enticing perfumes,
and touching their soft backs they simply moved
to other wildflowers, ignoring my presence.

Upon my hearing rests a pulsing current of sounds
as busy insects produce a noisy background,
the synchronous droning of cicadas in concert,
sounds familiar since the ears of childhood.

The heat of the day eddies upon everything near,
and the toasting smell of ripening grain
enriches the air deeply, and I breathe in that sweetness,
my walking effortless within fragrances balm.

MY FATHER'S HATS

In my father's closet were felt hats,
the best dress hats in covered boxes;
others were shelved for easy access,
each possessing its own personality
once coming to rest on his head.

He wore his hats as if nature intended,
and they appeared to belong there,
set at an angle he always favored.
When his genetic balding began
they offered some refuge or denial.

As one of our town's best-dressed men
a hat was chosen according to the occasion,
whether for work, church or social function.
At home he gardened with his head covered,
choosing one of the older hats to wear.
.
When I was young it required a chair
to reach the shelf with the dress hats,
and standing in front of the hall mirror
with a hat resting below my ears and eyes,
I was impressed how grown up I looked.

BOY SOPRANO

He was blessed to be a gifted boy soprano,
but given too brief a time of accolades,
singing lead in school operettas,
holding lyrics he remembers fondly.

He can still recall the heady feeling
when the school community applauded,
and was perfectly content in believing
that a charmed future awaited him.

He could picture himself on the silver screen
singing face to face with a lovely starlet,
and she looking at him with adoring eyes,
marveling at his rendition of "Beautiful Dreamer."

Over the next six months something happened,
and it seemed he was being redesigned;
there were those advising him to shave,
and he noticed more of the treble notes
were falling out of his voice range.

Within all too short a time frame
he was singing baritone in the chorus.

WITHIN THE POND

The placid pond stirs suddenly,
turbulence spinning up from deep places,
concentric ripples expanding on a journey
defining and sculpting the pond's dimensions.

I wonder what force channeled through these waters,
hidden from sight except in what I know.
Prey and predator fish cycle their lives here,
a giant water bug can siphon a frog in minutes.

In those spaces where choices are made
small fish still swim in hunger's pathways,
and when evening shadows lengthen
I will hear frogs sing their ancient hymns.

SHENANDOAH

Some days when I step into this lovely river,
it is with the feeling I can walk her surface,
then finding faith in intention inadequate,
I am quickly in the current's silky embrace
pulling at my knees as I walk the bottom rocks,
those older than time, belonging here or upriver.

I seek a known hole to drop deeper than eye line,
to feel more and hear better the river's voice,
and capturing the vision that I seek
to become a part of the timeless Shenandoah,
and in the pulsing of her sparkling waters
find the ancient wisdom of spiritual grace.

WALLET OF A YOUNG MAN

In Memory of J.O. Corell

This old wallet I hold, once war-weary,
settled on the hip of the young man walking,
a sad but homeward journey, the conflict over,
travel on foot away from prison life,
the horrors of Point Lookout, and before,
remembering fields of dying young men.

After the Potomac he crossed the Blue Ridge
to reach the Valley of the Shenandoah
that would be his guiding path to Tazewell,
but first weeks of more walking lay ahead,
through a countryside defaced, impoverished by war.

He found a measure of healing from strangers,
and some renewal of youthful spirit
in meager food offered, resting places given,
and he opened this wallet, empty of money,
holding a few thin papers from where he had been,
read the worn letter from home, his gift to share.

LOUDOUN VALLEY

Deeply embedded in dreams' recalling
just over a hill and a road winding,
a view so timeless and poignant
that when years pass with absence doubt,
I must travel back to see it again.

The road crests over the Catoctin hills
then enters the verdant Loudoun Valley,
in all its fertile and enchanting beauty,
spreading and reaching to the blue ridges
of the distant gentle mountains framing.

No matter the years or miles away
past grieving in so many passing,
those people most loved no longer here,
the view from the old road reassures me,
never leaving memory's recalling.

The tranquil feeling of beauty known,
in timeless sharing with others now,
embracing the view in mind or sight,
neither to be buried or lost to change,
nor will I ever tire of my lovely valley.

ROCK OF MYSTERIES

I've found a splendid rock to rest on,
hard as granite and gently sloping,
here forever, rooted to mountain.
Knowing which turns of path it follows,
my steps always quicken on approach,
from walking on challenging ridge lines
I find this smooth flat contour welcome.

Viewing the valley Shenandoah
confirms this as a perfect vantage,
and I think of secrets this rock holds,
my thoughts quickening in solitude.

Surely it was known by forest dwellers
who found this a perfect resting place,
perhaps a spiritual rock for some.
Pulpit like stone, here a tribal chief
could have held council with followers
while keeping watch of the western view.

Early settlers who farmed the lands east,
having displaced the forest people,
would find this pinnacle's vantage site
a watch tower for those forced westward.

Wide and smooth enough, this rock of secrets
may have been chosen for romantic moods,
when nights were warm, with a full moon's blessing.
At times in the stone's unremembered past
others may have come here seeking healing,
contemplating life and what lies beyond.

I wonder if there have been years and more
when no one came to this sentinel rock.
On a day of autumn hiking, viewing,
sitting here, singing full voice, I listen
to hear its echo off distant ridges,
enhanced in the journey returning back,
my song of faith for the gifts of today.

A DOG'S DEFENSE

Being loved with every need met,
I am genetically in pack comfort.
While years have passed not losing you,
separation remains my greatest fear.

I know you by touch and sound of voice,
but keeping you in view reassures most.
I am childlike at times, endearingly so,
trying to be better for you my defense.

When left alone, hours seem forever,
and I forget manners you've taught,
searching for you in everything within reach,
begging you to understand my anxiety.

I can't look for you beyond these rooms,
the door marking your leaving tightly closed.
If you return I will greet and forgive you,
hoping you overlook what I've done again.

A BIRD'S PLAINTIVE SONG

A bird's plaintive song has windows
through which I speak in a whisper,
and the morning brings awareness
to believe within a beating heart
a restless spirit finds a home.

Owning no dimensions,
time or place not confining,
and I've wondered on that journey,
for a spirit resides as it pleases.

For what reason the birds sing
than to welcome the morning light;
escaping the night's empty hours,
to be heard is the gift they bring.

In either wistful or glad songs
I hear remembered voices.

FRAGILE KITTEN

This fragile kitten I hold,
abandoned, just found,
odds so lacking, only skin and bones,
brought to me for healing.

Someone's neglect, roadside dropped,
and little chance with traffic speeding,
but today's hero not too busy to stop.
"Couldn't just leave it there," he said.

This bearded young man,
hobbling on his metal cane
did not speak of his time in combat,
only starving kittens he had rescued,
nursed to life, and sad to leave them,
not allowed to bring his orphans home.

His wounds though healed, had been severe,
his words now all about saving lives,
and today his focus on a little gray kitten.
"Life is precious, every ounce" he said,
"just have to give back, as I've received."

"We'll do our best" I assured him,
"she needs fluids, warming up,
gentle nursing care, whatever it takes,
and in your words, so well put,
life is precious, every ounce."

DRAFT HORSES

Gertrude and Bessie were a pair of draft horses,
and being around them, watching them work,
observing them at rest, or faces in the grain bucket,
I felt admiration, and the quietude of intimidation.

Their hooves were massive, and feathered above,
and they considered my offerings with dignity,
soft velvet muzzles taking carrots from my small hands.
Powerful muscles carried them effortlessly,
when pulling the plow or other heavy chores.

Their movements in the stalls belied their roles,
out of harness, they owned their space and regally stood,
one hoof up, at rest, moving only when they chose,
their pleasure of home within the quiet of barn walls.

They enjoyed the comfort from sweet feed in their bellies,
neither admiring or regretting the newly bought John Deere.

LIMERICK LADY

We were sent by the inn keeper
finding our way through roundabouts,
driving the few kilometers to Limerick city.
We stepped off the street into the hardware store,
and were greeted by a lady in working apron
who daily saw mostly people she knew,
recognizing we were strangers.

A brief exchange about what we needed,
then she asked where in America we lived,
speaking of family who lived in the states
saying someday she planned to visit.
She turned to her shelves behind a crowded counter,
and after a thorough search, said with regret,
she was unable to find the item we sought.

She spoke to a customer she called by name
to mind the store, she would briefly be gone.
Turning to us with an easy smile
asking that we follow her out the door,
that she was taking us to McKenna's store.

A briskly walked four blocks through a soft rain,
then after a neighborly chat with the store's owner,
she apologized for our trouble and turned to go.
We thanked her for her kindness, exchanging goodbyes,
and though we had heard of warm Irish welcomes,
wondering the truth of Ce'ad Mile Failte,
there was never a doubt after our Limerick lady.

GARDEN SYMMETRY

Walking through the symmetry of this garden
I marvel at the designed beauty of plant spacing,
and breathing the rising fragrance of the boxwood
sense a musty ageless familiarity here.

I pass at leisure through corridors of green,
patterns of grooming defining pathways,
and embroidered between brick and greenery
sequences of blending floral plantings,
tapestries of yellows, pinks and reds.

The garden reminds me there was first a vision,
then a commitment of time and labor,
and amid all of the defining loveliness
I think of God and man at work together.

STARTLING PHEASANT

There is a feeling of shock, when sudden sounds startle,
and I have been vulnerable to the unexpected,
hearing that which disquiets my equilibrium, altering stability,
being caught totally unsuspecting, unprepared.
There have been sounds that arrived softly, still disconcerting,
and I have strained to find the source of those intrusions.
Other times a sound is overwhelming, quick in a quiet place,
and my response is physical, tilting on the surrounding air.

On a cold November morning, walking through a field of stubble,
watching the woods that bordered, my footsteps the only sounds,
constant and familiar, becoming more unnoticed than not.
A walk when the day seemed timeless, horizons opening wide,
and my mind wandering, thinking about whatever presented,
the leaves and green now gone from trees and fields,
the woods wearing the silence of grays and browns,
and I felt the transition, earth becoming dormant.

Immersed in thought, aware of no other presence,
when a thundering sound came suddenly upon me,
and I was startled and swayed in my walking to
abruptly stop.
Quickly turning I saw the rising of a large pheasant,
out of the close brambles between field and trees
lifting upward on drumming wings flying into border woods,
crying out "Kok," "Kok," "Kok" in shrill appeal to
unseen others,
leaving my pulse accelerating, ears stunned, mind
appraising,
believing on balance, I was the more startled.

OCTOBER SURPRISE

A snowfall arrives as an unexpected surprise
upon October colors of our southern mountains,
silently and softly coming in the night,
leaving a white frosting adhering every surface.

I wake to find the morning of a bright new day,
and looking now from our hilltop perspective,
the roofs of near houses wear blankets of white
beneath rising gray wisps of wood-fire smoke.

The firs and pines shape the embroidery best,
snow on green boughs suggesting another season,
and I mentally consider if its December already,
but the stolid old maples still hold their leaves.

The autumn colors have enhanced intensity,
above the snow-covered ground and shrubs,
reds, yellows and burnt orange leap out,
and I am captivated by surrounding contrasts.

The sky hides within broken wind-rent clouds,
and beneath those gray folds disjointing now,
birds fly hurriedly seeking yesterday's earth,
feathers ruffled, heads tucked against the cold.

Our bird feeders are more for our pleasure
on fair sky days when the earth is warm,
but today they will save birds we've known,
and others will come once the welcome is told.

STONE FENCE

The feel of stone layered in this wall
is substantial, always cooler than the day,
challenging my sensitivity,
unlike touching a tree, feeling life therein,
coursing of fluids in expanding wood,
past and present palpably known.

Pressing my palms upon these gathered stones
perception arrives in different measure,
bringing thoughts of that which outlasts life;
choosing to sit atop this ageless wall
I take pause upon the autumn day,
browsing time and meaning of belonging.

A VIOLIN'S VOICE

I wish my voice were sweet as the violin,
singing with ease in notes low to high,
reaching all with effortless aplomb,
bridging half tones, all that lay between,
to sing as long as the audience stayed.

Looking at grandfather's old violin
I think how gifted the violin maker,
though gifting now who holds the bow.

It remains my secret wish
to have an inside chair upon the stage,
holding a polished violin just so,
sitting within the cascading sounds,
and when comes the last crescendo
pluck the strings while the cymbals clash.

FELINE BEHAVIOR

Watching the young kitten learning,
endless hours with deep sleep interludes,
no mother teaching, no example given.

Ten weeks old this orphan, human nurtured,
and I see genes working, gifting,
within this small gray tabby.

Instincts I've observed in cats suggest
the theory of collective unconscious
was postulated observing feline behavior.

The low profile creeping upon toy mouse,
stalking, with eyes and ears measuring,
the sudden pounce, quick neck grab
anchoring on, front claws piercing.

No role model for this kitten to follow,
only behavior bequeathed in the gene pool.
Not all knowledge is taught in books.

AFTERNOON IN A GREEN FIELD

The distant field enclosed by woods,
a shining green embroidered hill,
and I was drawn by sun and youth
to walk and rest its fragrant grass.

At the lone house on the narrow road
I chose not to request permission,
denial a risk, or being known.
The area I knew, but not that place,
nor who its owner or tenants were.

I walked uphill on a logging road
with years of overgrowth returning,
into woods becoming darkly dense,
beneath canopies of hardwood trees
reaching skyward, noon sunlight dimming.

An hour's walk through closeted spaces
until I reached the open green field,
and stepping into sunshine's graces
that felt a new day's fresh beginning.

I walked freely beyond trees' shadows,
savored caress of waving high grass,
then sitting down, became lost to time,
finding solitude, a sense of peace.

The hill faced south beneath a cloudless sky,
and freed for sun's warmth, lay on my clothing,
alone with birds' songs, humming of insects,
finding sleep's favor, undisturbed for hours.

I was awakened by a falling sun,
prompting my leaving as woods grew darker,
thinking of gifts in doing simple things,
hikes to bright hills, of sudden impulses.

CARILLON IN BYRD PARK

Early years of visiting cities consisted of day trips,
and I remember the constant current of noise,
high and low, over riding sounds never ceasing,
and we walked in an envelope of conversation,
adding little to the cacophony of clamor.

There may have been a nearby city carillon,
but I never heard the sound of cultured bells.
Not until college did I first hear them,
and then during a quiet evening of study
I heard bells ringing from a near distance,
and enthralled, wondered the source.

The next morning, a bright autumn beginning,
and out walking through the glories of maples
I heard the bells again, ringing an old hymn,
drawing me nearer to their location,
until I stood mesmerized at the carillon,
thinking how perfect those sounds,
how purely struck the musical notes.

I made time for them while living nearby;
now missing their ringing, years away.

THIS WATAUGA

Falling between wooded hills,
dropping quickly in race over broken rock,
in sweeping turns through wider places
the river pares earth from stone,
finding its path, forever following,
seeking the leading waters just ahead.

Owning large boulders that always were,
and quiet pools that favor wading within,
musical siren in its tumbling chase,
this Watauga, not knowing its appeal,
nor that I stand in its seductive waters
absent of any thought of changing this day.

HILL TOP HEALING

When seeking solitude for understanding,
life's complexities demanding,
I leave voices of roads and others,
distractions that obligate thoughts.

I journey time or miles to find quiet refuge
in hill high meadows, on mountain balds,
where wildflowers wave above deep grasses
in weaving undulations on caressing winds.

The fragrance off the breathing fields
grounds me to a renewed belonging,
and I am persuaded to find horizons of mind
where memory consents to comprehension.

PART THREE

AN ORIOLE NEST

I feel winter in my sitting beneath the locust tree,
looking upward through webs of leafless branches
to find the remnants of the orioles' past nesting,
their briefly used home from egg laying to fly aways,
wondering if they will return on the winds of March.

It was the second spring for the pair last year,
and we were proud they remembered from before,
when they first flirted, singing on spring's rising warmth,
mating and declaring their love as forever
to begin building their basket nest, unique to us.

The tree's limbs near the house for easy watching,
the orioles' feathers brightened two springs,
and when the egg sitting began, we waited too,
with anticipation that precedes the magic of birth,
checking frequently from our viewing window.

I remember sensing the excitement of the orioles
when the eggs hatched, hungry mouths emerging.
It would only be weeks before they left this nest,
and I wondered then, and since their leaving,
were they strong enough, those wings of fledglings.

I think of surviving the risks of foraging on their own,
how much of necessity did they learn and keep,
the teaching time seemed so brief from the parent pair,
and wonder who will fly in on the warmth of spring,
believing the nest needs only minor repairing?

REHOBETH

Remembering a Rehobeth summer
with family, and friends of my early youth,
and that July the water was chilling,
the waves welcoming, then knocking us down,
enlarging the fun, the sense of danger.

It was colder than the calendar suggested,
the adults sitting in canvas chairs, called us near
when we were too brave or the surf too rough.
They laughed that our knees were blue with cold,
wrapping us in towels when our lips turned purple.

Lying on the beach, feeling the earth shake
as coast guard batteries along the coast
fired shells into the Atlantic, practice or targeting,
and the year was 1942, when German submarines
prowled the ocean attacking vulnerable ships.

The effect was mildly jarring to a young boy
with thoughts always running ahead of events,
and my ears heard more than was expected
of fathers talking, concern quickening their voices,
where the war was fought, and place names so
strange.

My imagination knew no limits,
and I recall no fear of daylight waves,
but night walks on the beach were not benign,
the black ocean awake with frightening sounds
holding some awful mystery deep within.

REMEMBERING AN UNCLE

In memory of Bernard Kelley

His voice still rings in my memory,
higher in pitch than would be expected,
he being a barrel-chested dairy man
who could pitch hay bales as if weightless,
and hold a calf for steering with ease.

I called him Uncle Bernard, in friendship,
not being his nephew or other relation,
unless my cousins married his cousins,
then perhaps cousins twice removed,
and in our rural county that was possible.
It was more his son was my friend,
and I never tired of his many retold stories.

When we were still young, but old enough,
he would ask us to try his homemade wines
of which the parsnip, clear as amber sherry,
and the damson, his dark wine
as he called it, were the favorites.
We enjoyed the wine tasting in his cool cellar,
feeling it when returning to upstairs heat.

He often told a story of curing distemper
that infected a kennel of the hunt club's hounds,
by stuffing feed salt down their throats,
gagging them, breaking up their congestion.
It was usually told along with the wine,
concluding when he said, "and that's the truth."

OLE MISERICK

In Memory of Lee Vandeventer

He rolled his cigarettes,
spilling tobacco in the making.
When he smoked one
it danced on his lower lip,
adhering there as if glued
as he talked and laughed.

Driving the old pickup truck
was his respite from the cows and milking.
Its floor boards wore holes and wide gaps,
and riding roads and fields with him
I watched potholes and corn stubble
slide inches beneath my feet.

His laugh was contagious,
even as he teased me without mercy.
My time with him on the farm
had unforgettable appeal.
I was the only nephew
he called "Ole Miserick".
What that meant I never asked.

FIRE CALL

It was usually a windy night,
within the deepening cold of winter,
and we would be shaken from sleeping
by a wailing siren above the wind's sound,
an alarming, lonely howl of danger.

The rising, falling call reached everyone,
and from our town and surrounding farms
volunteer firemen responded quickly.
Sometimes it was a house or chimney fire,
less often a barn or business in flames.

If it was more than local firemen could handle,
the call went out to neighboring towns.
Depending on strength and direction of wind,
we would hear the sirens in nearby towns responding,
the number a signal of how large the fire was.

I have never forgotten the pungent smoke of a house fire,
a mix from burning wood, furnishings and wet ashes,
nor a family looking on, faces of loss awareness.

JANNEY'S STORE

In memory of Asa Moore Janney

Sitting quietly on Lincoln's south edge
is a quaint little store and post office,
angled to the road frontage,
its steep steps crowding the narrow parking,
which made no difference before the traffic
when it was only locals stopping.

The Quaker meeting house of worship,
generations of families long gathering there,
a community's defining place, just beyond.
Modest homes line the one village road
which has paved over cow path bends.

Janney's was downhill from the old school,
a brisk lunch time walk and adventure.
We chose our soda pop from the box cooler,
adding peanuts or crackers to complete our meal,
in youthful high spirits coming and going.

Behind the store's counter was Asa Moore,
proprietor, postmaster and local historian,
whose tolerance for youth, and pervading good humor
were found in his smile and melodic voice,
giving the store all the ambiance it could hold.

I retain the memorable impression of thinking
he had the charisma for a much larger stage.

GENTLEMAN OF OUR TOWN

In memory of J.V. Nichols

He was easily recognized
this tall man walking downtown,
doing so with a confirmed dignity of posture,
dressed in a three-piece suit,
not often seen on our town's streets,
striking a figure like none other,
and old enough to be who he was.

His classroom was at roadside
where he sought to improve the youth
who too often walked with a slouch,
and he set a convincing example,
reminding us to hold our shoulders back
like him, to walk proud as Virginians,
and with that he had our attention,
and claimed the moment to talk on.

He knew most of us by name,
and would casually begin his lecture
about where first settlers had lived,
location of blacksmith, ice plant,
and he would talk of the great fire
burning the town's thriving business area.

I remember those homilies
amid the impatience of youth,
but thinking now of Mr. J.V.'s absence,
it is with a feeling of nostalgia.

How I would love to turn the calendar back,
see him approaching and bid me stay,
and hear him speak in his firm but kindly way,
"hold those shoulders back, young man."

SYMPHONY IN THE BARN

In memory of Ed Payne

I knew him as a nearby dairy farmer,
seeing him in town always dressed for work,
his speech slow and deliberate
with the rural Virginia drawl and accent
familiar to us, but often misunderstood
by those with more formal education.

On a call to his farm with the mentor of my youth,
who was there to treat a cow with milk fever,
we entered the barn to be greeted by the usual smells,
the pervasive bovine breath and waste,
and sweet and sour odor of ensilage.

Sounds of cows restless in stanchions,
but something more within those walls;
beautiful symphonic music over riding the rest,
from a dusty phonograph in a corner,
and I asked the farmer what was playing.

"The third movement of Beethoven's Fifth Symphony,"
and then he spoke about being a patron
of the National Symphony Orchestra,
and how much that was a part of his life.

I realized then that brogans wearing manure
and a farmer's country way of talking
do not define or restrict intellect or interest.

SHORT HILL FIRE TOWER

Riding the highest ridge within the valley
a fire tower stood sentinel to life below,
one of the daily defining points
reminding us where we lived.

Looking up to the ridgeline
brings mixed memories.
When young we climbed the tower
because it was there, in dare's way.

Reaching the top on adrenaline's push
we felt our distance above the tree line,
seeking villages and farmlands east
and views west to the horizon's Blue Ridge.

The shadows of the mountain
fall on the near village in early evening,
washing over granite stones
etched with names and dates.

A friend died near the tower,
and I've wondered if he climbed that day,
looking though shadows of the Short Hill
into the valley gray markers define.

IRIS AND DAYLILLIES

I accepted the offer, so kindly made,
she was gifted to be thoughtful.
We had sold the home place,
the house that cradled me from birth,
and perhaps she sensed my feeling of loss,
learning from my face more than words.

We walked the rooms together,
and I touched walls, the fireplace mantle,
looked out windows, opened every door
closing them with care and finality.

I alone went to the cellar to remember
our old coal-burning furnace,
and how much cleaner the oil furnace,
and everyone so proud with that transition.

I looked at shelves once holding hundreds of jars,
home-canned tomatoes, string beans, apple sauce,
apple butter, peaches, damson preserves, pickles,
all from our summer garden and local orchards.

I saw empty bushel baskets that held potatoes,
the crock where the combs of honey were stored,
and memories came flooding to my eyes,
and I was glad to be alone in that space.

Outside as we walked yard and garden
I spoke admiringly of my friendship with trees,
and how I loved the iris and day lilies,
reminding me of seasonal beginnings.

I expected nothing except allowance of time,
walking the ground holding so many memories,
when she asked me to come back the next morning
for one more visit before leaving.

The next day I returned, to be surprised by gifts,
iris rhizomes and clumps of day lilies,
and they have continued giving and expanding
more than five hundred miles from home.

I accept great pleasure in their beauty
thankful always for the thoughtful giving,
reminding me daily of so much more.

FINDING PATIENCE

I sit in shadows of the willow weeping
dripping still from morning dew,
keen to be here in the day's first stirrings,
alert to birds above, swirl of fish below
in the gentle creek's quiet ripples.
I discover patience here infusing my day,
nurturing the best version of myself.

Upon this defining a hill gives morning shade,
where I often climb to its highest clearing,
just below trees that frame the ridgeline,
to claim the viewing across rolling fields
and beyond to blue in ridges west,
those mountains that frame my daily belonging,
discovering patience from seasons passing.

GOLDEN MOMENTS

I walk the beach as the sun is setting,
white gulls diving over an incoming tide,
and sandpipers chasing the frothy edges.

Looking nowhere and everywhere
absorbed in reflections on the day,
when suddenly sky and water turn golden,
and I stop to embrace these gifting moments.

Asking it to last, while calling to others,
hoping it will wait, this must be shared,
the others will come if I can find them.

DAWN AT TYBEE PIER

I walk the pier, a crescent moon riding high
giving what little light reaches these boards,
as waves below drum on the vacant beach,
the ocean holding mystery at this dark hour.

Timing is what truly matters when chasing the dawn,
and as I look east, eyes tearing in the onshore wind,
sky and water seem to intersect in the dark,
meshing and losing their separate identities,
and I am glad to be here before first light.

I have a solitary mindset, not a lonely feeling,
although no one else is keeping early watch.
For a time, the sky remains locked to light,
and I have a fleeting feeling the time is wrong,
but keep my eyes focused on that far off place
where dark water, wind and sky are waiting.

First light comes on the horizon's edge
lifting into view by earth's rotation,
spreading slowly in a thin line north and south,
and after an interlude, brings exquisite colors
violets, blues, oranges and reds paint the sky.
It must be seen now; it does not wait.

The glories of morning's birth are brief,
and although I will carry this sunrise with me,
soon the morning sun will climb, claiming the day,
while fisher gulls challenge water and sky,
and I will watch them feeding gladly in the light.

NIGHT OF FULL MOON

Tonight the moon is full and expansive,
the beach stares the distant horizon
brought nearer on pathways of light.
The hours of the moon's rising defy time,
and I watch my children run through moon beams,
the sand pale beneath their small, quick feet.

On this night the ocean harbors fewer secrets,
while the young at play haunt my mood,
believing we are here in a forgotten place,
dark of night beyond the farthest view,
missing sun painting the moon, touching all I know,
and what I see seems older than time.

ARTIST ON THE SQUARE

It was mid-morning on the sun dappled square,
and pausing my walk to watch an artist paint
making soft brush strokes on canvas,
and nothing seemed quite serious enough.

The artist smiling, relaxed, taking paint to brush,
then brush applied with conceived effect,
scattered colors, nothing more at first,
and I surmised something would come of it.

Others there as well, curious or knowing,
and I whiled my time in anticipation,
distracted by thoughts of how beauty is found,
doubting that an artist could do that with ease.

I wondered to what creation she was committed,
and would the art be impressionist or abstract.
Bemused, I turned away to speak to a stranger,
and we became engaged in yesterday's news,
my thoughts distracted from the work in process
finding differing perspectives on the spring day.

After some time, I turned back to the artist
to observe beauty of color and form emerging,
and although the canvas still early in progress
I found an April morning being reborn,
azaleas in the square, dewy fresh and pink,
live oaks above, Spanish moss draping,
those of us standing near, just as we were,
and Savannah preserved in her loveliest hour.

WALKING DONEGAL

I cannot look enough upon the green hills,
walking this stone-flanked narrow road,
and sheep marked with splashes of paint
focused ahead in passing by.

Their aged shepherd follows behind,
blackthorn stick supporting steps,
his border collie among woolly bodies,
doing the herding, prodding them on.

I speak to man and dog, looking at the man,
thinking it might interest him to talk,
those must be tedious hours with only dog and sheep.
He nods, his lips moving as if in prayer,
passing by, keeping pace with the others.

I am enthralled by the surrounding hills,
wind-blown grass and ancient rock,
while it doesn't seem he gives an upward glance,
and I wonder if he feels the beauty of Donegal.

OFF PARKWAY TRAIL

This mountain trail I know,
never the same beyond its first turning,
and I begin beneath an open sky,
the sun passing thin shadows.

The path winds under dense canopies,
rocks and roots pausing progress
requiring more care in walking,
warming me in the effort.

A creek edges the trail in low places,
speaking softly, enriching solitude.
I rest and stare its moving waters
before embarking the next uphill climb.

Turnings of the trail come frequent,
what is familiar always changing,
and I feel at one with all that surrounds me,
finding reminders of past seasons' presence.

When rhododendron and laurel wore spring
I walked beneath a nearer sun;
wild daisies and asters flowered,
and I felt immersed in the breath of summer;
life in the forest was slowing down
as maples, hickory and river birch
announced vivid colors of autumn.

December finds me here again,
and I look beyond leafless mysteries,
sleeping woodlands quieter now,
and hidden during other seasons' abundance
long views the trail reveals,
the sky opening to farthest ridge lines,
and I go beyond where my eyes can see.

TO DOC WATSON

Blues from Deep Gap to mountains west,
his voice blessing what eyes couldn't see,
songs touching us deeply;
remembering
Lordy Lordy, hallelujah,
how that man could sing.

Gifting those who heard him sing,
his guitar coloring chosen lyrics,
framing his voice's mellow warmth;
remembering
Lordy Lordy, hallelujah,
how that man could sing.

BEST FRIENDS

For some, it is hard to understand
the depth of love between dog and man.
At times it may seem more one-sided
than what I have shared with my best friends.

Lili Belle, my loving Cavalier,
her childlike eyes stare to consume me,
finding acceptance upon my lap,
her feelings shown and well understood.

Pete, a Cocker Spaniel, likes to talk,
yodeling requests, ever patient.
He buries his face under my arm,
content in the pleasure of petting.

They look forward to our daily walks,
and I watch them exploring pathways,
their joy found in the simplest pleasures,
living only for one day's moments,
and that keeps me content and wiser.

NEW CALENDAR

In January I hang a new calendar
marking special dates of family, friends,
wondering about unexpected events,
spaces and pages innocent enough
offering a clean slate, new beginnings.

Before year's end that will change,
gray days seeking to control our lives,
better that more are bright.
If past years offer any wisdom,
we can't predict the future
times and seasons bringing change.

Month to month the pages announce
the first of this following the end of that,
where memories and expectations meet.
I often turn a page reluctantly,
having favorites, sad at the passing,
feeling something was missing.

I relish the first day of March
watching for robins and daffodils,
Autumn's cool days a refreshing change,
intense colors greeting morning frost,
while I am disappointed by December
if it doesn't bring an early snowfall.

Summer, a favorite of youth,
seems longer than necessary,
though I hope enough for my tomatoes.

MOUNTAIN SPRING

On edges of spring ascending
I sense the earth being reborn,
shedding short days of reluctant light,
the long sleep and dark hours of winter.

I find early awakening of the season
in opening of white dogwood leaves,
rosy pink display of our mountain red bud,
and beneath these, emerging larkspur and trillium
lifting through mulch of past autumns' debris.

Days still begin with chill mornings,
smoke from firewood burning where others live,
while a warmer sun quickens each succeeding day,
as spring in no haste climbs the mountain.

Dark places come alive upon that warmth,
and I walk in growing awareness of new life,
finding along every path fresh beginnings,
reminding me of promises unfolding.

DREAMS ESCAPING

I wait in the spreading shadows
as night's gathering hours arrive,
before the fitful, restless darkness
delays my sleep, then yielding to need
takes me to an uncharted dreamland,
where I am led down spiraling paths,
and into unplanned sudden meetings
with presence of faces long unseen.

I know my mind needs sleep,
its filing system vastly overloaded,
but I hope there will come a time
when a rewarding chase brings closure,
or I arrive in some familiar space,
finding on a new day's beginning
that with whom, or where I've been,
do not quickly chase from mind,
escaping my audience before the telling.

FINDING AN OTTER

I've watched two otters swimming here,
the creek runs slow in summer,
sometimes freezing over in winter,
but if there is late winter snow,
or now, March rains falling for days,
the creek spills into the field,
its water laced with debris,
the bridge not safe to cross.

Otters know things I don't-
their swimming effortless,
their lodges unknown to me,
and here may be one I've seen
swimming carefree, trusting instincts;
but as I hold this sleek-stilled body,
turning cold on hope leaving,
I cannot find outward reason.

Sudden loss deeply pains me,
and this lovely otter I think I knew,
overwhelmed in sudden flooding
within its element thought secure.

WANTING FOR LYRICS

Remembering years of gathering occasions
finding ourselves around the piano,
drawn there by one with talent,
long known and familiar selections.

By no signal we made our way
across the lively room, in high spirits,
an unspoken persuasion drawing us,
emboldened by the evening's refreshments.

Someone encouraged began the lyrics,
softly singing, beneath the piano's chords,
then another voice joined in, and more,
as timidity dissolved in the sharing.

I remember the best, and off-key voices,
the camaraderie of lusty singing,
but still regret we lacked a words person,
anyone to carry us through the song.

FALLING LEAVES

I watch leaves of September spiral down
coming to rest on the creek's quiet pool,
nearly imperceptible their turning
before being caught by unseen currents.

Their destiny to travel, first falling,
then floating on an uncertain journey,
powerless, except in their gold beauty,
be they maple, birch or river willow.

Leaves upon water mesh with others,
shoulder to shoulder enter ripples,
quickly pass through the noisy vortex
reaching pools to again swim alone.

At times I've felt like a falling leaf,
captive within surrounding currents,
then slipping fast in a downward pull
swim to haven in quiet waters.

SUMMERVILLE

On the lovely streets of Summerville
surrounding the old arsenal, now a college,
there is a refinement of quiet living,
a sense of refuge from daily work
with a nurturing leisure at day's end.

A place where neighbors are known
and families here for generations,
with space for walking at leisure safely
under the wide canopies of aged oaks,
and lawns adorned with seasonal flowers,
ablaze with colors of azaleas in spring.

The village developed on "the Hill,"
high above Augusta's riverside birth,
an escape from southern summer heat,
for shaded days and cooler nights.

The homes range from cottage to mansion,
with a strong work ethic prevailing.
A pleasant sociability is present,
a southern tradition of good manners,
the pleasure of community, feel of belonging.

PART FOUR

ANCHORING ROOTS

There is serenity in observing trees
knowing those anchoring roots dig deeply,
spreading out under my feet
unseen, not heard in their probing,
bringing lifeblood to trunk and limbs;
and I watch leaves sliding, turning
as the evening breeze has its way,
lifting, fanning, before the wind drops,
when only deeper green prevails.

Leafy branches hold the moment,
becalmed for short measure only,
then a stronger wind rustles through,
earth bound roots balancing the tree.
I feel that strength stirring far below
lifting upward into answering leaves,
reassuring voices to my hearing.

I am reminded how I am anchored
by all that I was taught, and learned.
There were times that brought challenges
when my turnings seemed aimless,
but nurtured within the cradle's hope
roots of self were planted deeply.

SELF DISCOVERY

The reality of self defines us,
a universe of ideas in motion,
filtering truth from all the rest.
I look back on a lifetime of discovery,
seeking and learning never ending,
encounters that bequeathed uniqueness.

Defining markings of who we are
decide the efficacy of our responding.
I have journeyed through a lifetime
finding, then losing concepts of beauty,
lately rediscovered with wisdom's sight,
more enchanting and daunting than ever.

.

FIRST SNOWFALL OF WINTER

All day I've watched the sky,
walking now beneath layered clouds,
appearing full, in silence waiting,
and sensing the air becoming still,
I step with expectation into that quietude
to hear the snow approaching.

It begins softly just beyond my reach,
moving out of the wood's near edges,
where I see white crystal flakes
against the tree line's gray face,
moving quickly and nearer to me
while the earth around has lost its voice.

Birds forget singing in flight to the woods,
singly and in companion pairs
seeking the trees protective warmth;
for there are nests that they know,
waiting homes in wooden faces,
and laurel patches dense and thick.

I resist an impulse to seek shelter,
for this first snow of winter
kindles old memories and feelings new,
and I will watch the hills turn white
until my steps become heavy,
or evening moves beyond twilight.

LIGHTS THROUGH SNOW

Today the sun's presence seems distant
lost in the depths of falling snow,
absent shadows enhancing quietude
enclosing on the afternoon's pale light.

I walk aware of familiar sounds missing,
snowflakes descending the only movement,
a day without wind, time becoming lost,
while the layered clouds close every horizon.

I see dim lights of our neighbor's windows,
their house hiding in the white enfolding,
only beaming squares in rows of two
prying, playing upon the fading view.

I sometimes stop for a visit when walking,
but decide to pass by this winter day
choosing not to pause for familiar talk,
thankful their lights pierce the falling snow.

EYES OF THE DEER

In the briefness of an eye blinking,
a deer caught in the headlights,
an antlered head above fearful eyes,
then the awful sound of impact.

We were nearing an intersection,
the wipers sweeping the snow away,
when out of the night's white darkness
the deer was briefly in the lights.

I braked to a stop, sliding on fallen snow,
afraid that beautiful animal lay dead,
or severely injured, suffering, in shock,
and I thought of fear seen in his eyes.

Getting out of the car, I looked around
finding empty roadsides of unblemished snow,
returned to the car's warmth to retrieve a light,
again finding only snow on winter ground.

Someone later said deer are tough, hard to kill,
kindling my hope he made it safe that night.
Another suggested the deer lay dying beyond my search,
and I remember that face of soulful eyes.

SUDDEN SUMMER STORM

My vantage point looking west,
from the near mountain's shadow,
thunderheads forming, climbing,
white tops riding black bottoms,
hosting gathering darkness.

I watch as trees catch the wind,
leaves' pale undersides turning,
weaving on darker shading,
scent of rain freshens the air
cooling deep summer's presence.

A brief calm moments before
thunder drums on lightning's flash,
lawn chairs rolled, legs to the sky,
rain drops riding gusts of wind,
in retreat I seek shelter.

Wet and chilled, but feeling more alive,
the years forgotten on wind and rain,
and I don't mind being young again.

HANDS WE HOLD

My child, your childhood
moves in memory's shadows.
When reaching for your hand
I think of your trusting touch,
searching for that soft small hand
that closed within my own;
too soon like birds taking flight
my hands have known goodbyes.

Feeling the poignancy of loss
even though years have passed,
I reconcile myself to the present,
thinking, this is your time,
too soon to miss your child's touch
those known, soft gifting hands.

Years that slip from our grasp
later bring hours of reminiscing,
when we think of hands closely held,
remembering the times of separation,
defining moments, both loss and gain.

HIS CHAIR

I sit in his chair, it always was,
and although I became taller,
it seemed he always sat higher,
and his wisdom, testing mine
through opinions sagely offered.

When I was very young, and he not old
my misplaced energies did not always please;
later I was young, and he older,
those difficult reproaches reversing.

Then I became older and he more so,
finding tolerance the years admit,
and he, in our time aging softly,
owned the day with utmost brevity,
sitting high, from his chair opining.

QUESTIONS IN THE JOURNEY

Every life owning infinite potential,
my journey toward a life of worth
began while framing questions,
moving beyond being absorbed in self.

That egocentricity gifted in survival genes
became baggage from the cradle carried too far,
and I think of so much time passing
before fully investing in paths to truth,
losing the center of the universe in doing so.

Gaining perceptions of what truly matters,
I found in the kingdom of ideas
that which enabled who I became,
a life contented in what I've learned,
satisfied not all questions need answering.

IN PROFILE ONLY

I thought I saw her sitting near,
smiling, gray hair, hands folded in her lap,
as I remembered how many years ago?

She seemed to be enjoying the moment,
with someone across from her,
relaxed at table, in casual conversation.

I couldn't find a way for her to see me,
moving to where she should,
only finding her always in profile.

She never turned or looked my way.
Though longing to get her attention,
I was mute to call her name.

WINDOWS ABOVE THE SNOW

A photograph challenging my imagination,
the house surrounded by heavy snow,
no footprints marring that pristine blanket,
and I look at windows, their empty darkness.

Believing someone, or more of those I knew
looking out from within those spaces,
and I strain to find them, their faces nearly seen,
just out of view of the camera's eye.

I wonder on that captured moment
preserved in the briefness of a shutter's wink,
if plans were being made for the day,
or had the overnight snow changed all.

I can imagine burning logs in the fireplace,
coffee on the stove, telephone calls
made to family and others about the storm,
inquiries about which roads can be traveled,
comparing notes about pantries,
not expecting mail or newspaper delivery.

If I could step into that captured time,
I would be glad for a book, loved ones near,
window view of snow, and what lay beyond.

THEIR PEW

It was their pew, the aging couple,
where no one else knowingly sat,
only an infrequent parishioner, or visitors
would occasionally claim that space.

They arrived earlier than most,
seeing them there was reassuring,
glad no reserved sign was needed.

There was a focused witness in their worship,
devoted attention to offered prayers,
and their reverence enriched our faith.

In the gathering room after Mass,
a warmth of greeting for everyone they met,
gifts of friendship to carry beyond,
remembered more than the homilist's words.

IN SPRING'S WARMTH

Your hands seem so cold.
I feel your grip slightly pressed,
light in your eyes grown dimmer.

You said the robins have not returned;
I asked if you could hear their singing.
Warmth of the sun is not like before.

I bring you a blanket.
Your sleep comes quick and deep,
while robins feed in lively pairs.

When you awaken they will be singing,
the sun grown warmer,
and you will speak again of your youth.

NO CAGE AS LOVELY

The cage too small for eager wings,
no enclosure could be large enough,
and all day long she sang a sad song,
we thought at first happy sounds.

A bird feeder by a window facing south,
and her days were spent watching others,
sensing their joy in a life in the open,
flying near, leaving on freedom wings.

On a warm summer day, the cage left open,
and escape found confining walls around,
frantically biding her time until a door opened
through which she flew, landing briefly in a tree.

I thought she could be persuaded to return,
but her choice was made on impatient wings,
a pausing glance back to me, keeper pleading,
then up and away, I watched her soaring flight.

My feelings of regret, though no misunderstanding,
for flight is a lovely gift, the passion of being free;
wishing safe travel, her kind somewhere beyond,
standing transfixed until I could no longer see.

YOUR FACE

I am entranced by facial expressions,
looking closely to find truth and hope
believing they are the best gifts we wear.

A perfect chin isn't important,
finding no regret in shape of nose,
but discover beauty where I focus most,
in eyes that brighten in laughter,
upward turn of smiling lips,
faint blush rising unaware.

The rest doesn't matter at all,
a heart is won on beauty's innocence.

WINTER WIND

I listen to the wind of winter howling
as it tries to find edges to prey upon,
corners of the old frame house shake
deflecting what they can, absorbing some,
and I've felt that on nights like this
enough to rock the house back and forth,
yielding to the strong northwest gusts.

Somewhere a power line went down,
perhaps a broken tree's falling,
the lights flickered twice and were gone,
and we feel vulnerable in their absence.
I've lit candles to keep the watch,
their flames dancing in this drafty room,
to and fro on invading currents.

I feel a refugee in a confined space,
believing the wind tonight a living thing,
a willful pulling on boards and nails
wanting to break through walls or roof,
and I move my chair from its window view.

No night for a wood fire, or restful sleep,
keeping watch, listening to wind on wood,
trusting in mortar and stone foundation.

THAMES WATCHING

Somewhere in this river's past
of aging docks and poets' songs,
even now in faces seen
part of my genetics sleeps,
or walks nearby in its watch.

The Thames rolls by and out to sea
knowing empire claimed and gone,
tolled forever in city bells,
red and black and shades between,
if they exist, it would be London.

Royals' frolics dwell on lips,
Cromwell's crimes in dusty books,
Saint Paul's standing through the blitz,
the Bard's words still live today;
remains that resourceful strength
being English, nothing more.

WHITEOUT

My headlights pierce the swirling snow,
and I search for the road lost in white,
blowing snow slanting across the Catoctins,
unbroken in sameness, no edges tonight.

My car digs a tunnel that quickly closes,
and I sit forward, hands tightly steering,
straining wipers sweeping the narrow view,
travel becoming claustrophobic,
and I feel a lost traveler tonight.

Recalling I set out without thinking,
in the comfort of driving this road before,
now wishing to have someone with me,
although only the foolish are out tonight.

If I meet another car in this whiteout,
I'll wave the driver to stop,
perhaps we can talk, wait out the storm.
Surely anyone would agree to that,
two lonely travelers on the road tonight.

DEAR FRIENDS

Two dogs that blessed my adult years
were abandoned on roadsides.
Maeve, a small spaniel, black and white,
was brought to the clinic, thin, infected skin,
hairless in large areas, her tail denuded,
suffering from generalized mange.

In spite of her condition, neglect of someone,
her tail wagged in friendly greeting,
and the will to live brightened her eyes,
spaniel sad and glad at the same time.

She healed following months of treatment,
and became a member of our family.
a friend to all, holding no enmity,
loving all from grandparents to grandchildren,
and her expanded name of Maevy Gravy
speaks easily to our affection for her.

Pepita was found on a country road,
brought to our clinic one morning,
ten weeks old by estimate.
She suffered from a viral disease
affecting her nervous system,
leaving her with a stilted gait,
wearing a questioning smile.

She had a mixed breed's easy temperament,
was accepted and mentored by Maeve,
growing rapidly into a large body.
She played games with keen focus
that overcame her balance problems.

Maeve and Pepita were each unique,
and a source of joy for many years,
though their time with us seemed all too brief.

OBELISK

Within the night's darkest hour,
into the depths of sleep's realm,
comes an unsettling dream recurring,
a piercing light with focused beam
transits from a tall and perfect obelisk,
chasing the blackness, searching for me.

That looming tower of silver walls
dominant to every thought I hold,
standing alone on a glassy plain
nothing broken in that broad expanse,
stretching on in distant sameness
beyond the edges of my dream's reach.

All I can see has perfect design,
obelisk, the plain stretching forever,
the light that never wavers or bends;
and I am not content with perception
hovering far beyond my understanding.

Into that time of sleep's awareness,
out of the darkest and farthest corner
comes suddenly upon the shining plain,
an unwieldy, unraveling sphere
uninvited, unwelcome, altering all.

A strong voice commands to act quickly,
and I run breathless upon the plain
trying, but failing to reach the intruder,
chasing forever that wobbling sphere,
unable to recover perfection's simplicity,
before the light in the obelisk disappears.

PREDICTABILITY

They could have been miles apart,
distance not inhibiting their intimacy of thought,
knowing the other's perceptions
on any matter, anything to be considered.

Their response was not the same,
he, always more analytical and precise,
she, having to excuse and repair so often
saw the bigger picture more easily.

The beauty of it was they understood
each other's predictability of response,
not so much compromising as accepting.
A lifetime spent together carried that gift.

THE GIFTING TREE

Under spreading limbs of the hillside oak,
my favorite place when seeking solitude,
and having been here many times
I sit with my previous presence felt,
to gaze the meadow bending down the hill
in southeastern slant to morning sun.

My farmer friend, if he happens by,
will not take surprise, I'm so often here.
He once asked about my health,
and I spoke of the tree as a healing place.
If he sees me now, he will wave and pass,
leaving the quiet unbroken that time will fill.

Always a stirring breeze turning summer leaves,
and in winter, I study the webbed branches,
leaves come and go, limbs keep the memory known.
This is a tree much older than farm or me,
respected, left standing when clearing was done.

LIFTING WIND

Standing on this shelf of weathered rock,
sentinel to wind blowing up the mountain,
I feel it lifting away the summer heat,
braced in open stance to the rising current,
finding the need to anchor myself.

Stepping close to the ledge's edge,
I bring offerings to challenge the wind,
throwing them over and down
toward the tree tops far below,
watching them chase back above me.

Becoming unsteady, in vertigo's grasp,
I think briefly of another step,
to join the wind, like a feather, a leaf,
lifted far above, rising far beyond.

WALK THROUGH THE ORCHARD

The season of the apple harvest come and gone,
we walk the naked orchard row by row
seeing blackbirds on limbs where apples hung.

The ground beneath my feet soft from frost melt,
and I feel a new season approaching,
weeks and months when earth falls asleep,
at times to know only long melancholy nights.

Remembering childhood, sunshine in every day,
but I can't think which trees matured the Winesaps,
or where the sweet Grimes Golden ripened.

My friend walks with me, four legs worse than my two,
and I hope he goes first, although not soon,
never to understand if he loses me.

DOG WALKS

His enthusiasm never diminishes,
in prancing expectation, laughing face,
impatient about my fumbling hands;
getting harness on, leash secure,
keys jingle, door opens, closes,
we're off, his focus led by scents.

He must know it will be the same walk,
like the day before, and many preceding,
but the grassy areas, the shrubs nearby
still hold surprises for his keen nose.

He checks on me, looking over his shoulder,
stops countless times for marking,
and I stay connected through pauses,
and sudden detours of impulsive curiosity.

He may wonder why I'm so upright,
no way to enjoy the same pleasures
without my nose exploring the ground.

FEARS IN THE DARK

When do we first find fear in living?
I wonder if it is caught in infancy,
or earlier within the mother's womb
when that secure and nurturing space
feels the onset of sudden danger.

I've walked through dark tree tunnels
hearing night sounds chilling, threatening,
and watched the eerie dance of bats,
darting around on tilting wings,
flying closer, nearer to my kindling fears,
for far too many fables I've been told.

Within the old frame farmhouse,
moaning and groaning of wood and wind,
a night without light from lamp or sky,
and in the same sleeping room
that will seem so inviting, so safe
when come the birth of daybreak and morning sun,
now holds a blackness dense and blinding,
and I feel vulnerable in the unbroken dark;

and wonder again of in the womb life,
what is sensed there, how much is felt?

.

PANSIES IN WINTER

Overnight cold winds and snow
pushed our pansies faces down,
early morning's frigid air
holds them chilled and drooping still.

I am intrigued with wonder
how they manage to survive,
while other bold-stemmed flowers
gave up with the early frost,
and will not be seen again,
until spring's replanting days.

I trust the sun's mid-day warmth
will suffice, rekindling life,
warming the drowsing pansies
to rise above winter's grasp,
and soldier on as before
with vibrant, funny faces.

YELLOW MAPLE

I look across two yards from my window on autumn,
and see the loveliest maple in glorious yellow,
wishing that tree were mine, and not his by chance.

Nothing else in that yard bears resemblance to beauty,
and the tree is of a previous owner's choosing;
now the best in the neighborhood stands there,
lacking evidence of any resident pride.

Yesterday, he was complaining to me and another
that when those yellow leaves fall to the ground,
he hoped they would blow somewhere else,
hinting that a chain saw would be a better choice.

I believe fallen leaves on that unkempt lawn
will beautify even when gold colors fade,
hoping the wind from the west will bypass his wish,
the maple still standing for next year's autumn.

DACHAU JOURNEY

We rode a fast modern train
out from the old city of Munich,
through an autumn countryside
prospering beyond our windows.

We were on a pilgrimage to Dachau,
where seventy years earlier
people were forced to make this trip
riding cramped in cattle cars,
into a future dark, without hope.

Leaving the train at Dachau station,
we walked under a heavy gray sky
that carried a chilling October rain,
down a silent street that brought us
to the entrance of the grounds of shame.

The welcoming gates still held the lie
"Arbeit Macht Frei"
(Labor makes you free).

The tragedy at Dachau overwhelmed us,
and our thoughts were of those innocents
who entered the gates, to suffer and die,
an evil far beyond history's telling.

Learning about what happened there
we offered prayers for all the dead,
yet found no answer to the question;

"Where were you?"

FALL OF A SILVER MAPLE

The sky torn in half by yellow fire,
below its wrath my silver maple
grounded upon space its shadow knew;
years since, I can see that falling tree.

I do not recall discordant sound,
lost echoes ripple beneath knowing,
only condemning the lightning's flash
that brought a majestic maple down.

GARDEN DAWNING

I step into the breath of early morning,
bare feet waking on the cool dew,
sensing remnants of night,
the hour shrouded and silent.

While my garden holds scant light,
seeming gray with disinterest in waiting,
I look east, far beyond tree tops,
to see the sun climb a summer dawning.

I watch light slowly bring shaded colors,
familiar shapes and contrasts emerging,
and riding the spreading illumination
bird songs welcome the early day.

Unlike inaccessible night dreams
I reach out to touch beauty,
and dipping my fingers into a damp rose
brush that wine to my lips.

The sweetness of the moment defies words,
the clock ticking the only sound I fear.

SAYING GOOD-BY

On every occasion of saying good-by,
sometimes all too briefly done,
there is something more to say,
asking you to wait just a little longer.

I need your leaving delayed,
to impart some wisdom of caring's grace;
finding it difficult to accept separation
whenever a loved one leaves.

Did I tell you about turns in the road
making decisions about good and what's not,
never letting anyone possess you,
that sharing as equals enriches our lives?
I want you to be the best you can be,
wishing every pain fleeting, every joy lasting.

Most of all I need to say I love you,
hope and faith are built from within,
take them along in your every journey.

HIGH WATER BRIDGE

The old bridge is gone now, torn down,
the one with character, trestles and charm,
with one-way traffic and a politeness
of slow approaches, slower crossings,
time for a waving hello, and thank you,
with courtesy to another to cross first.

It was a narrow bridge with history,
ours, other travelers, its own shared.
Four walkers could cross abreast with ease,
and the distance from home to bridge
family famous for being the 'long dog walk.'

A familiar landmark built as a high bridge
above waters of the ancient New River,
at times overflowing with rapid snowmelt,
or more often mountain rains lasting for days.

The new bridge two lanes wide and generic,
lacking pot holes or girders overhead,
missing those occasions of courtesy
when no one seemed to be in a hurry.

PART FIVE

THE MONUMENT

A monument erected for the beholder,
standing on a manicured expanse of lawn
with sculpted shrubs, beds of flowers,
a lovely place for thinking what lies beyond.
In the distance the mountains of blue ridges
holding centuries of blessings in gentle folds,
frame the marker, starkly obtrusive.

It seemed a touching approbation,
with name, dates, a verse that he was loved,
and for those years of widowhood,
the daily reminder of a shared life for her,
now resting in a nearby churchyard.

The new family wants him there too,
but there is that formal trust of perpetuity,
the stony tribute to a man they never knew,
resented in its unrelenting presence.

On gray days when mountains turn black,
the white monument seems to edge closer,
affecting the delicate nature of the lady of the house,
and there is quiet talk of an accidental incident,
the demise of that enduring ornamentation.

AN EVENING WALK

Every house on this street
is home to people that I know,
some better or longer than others,
and those that are most familiar
are the thresholds I've crossed.

It's easy in this night of walking
to see which neighbors are out,
or those that are in known rooms.
The brick house with porch light on
confirms our friends' absence,
I'm sure only for the evening,
if for longer, we would have heard.

The corner house on the right,
with every window owning a lighted room,
as the young couple have guests tonight,
the house looking so alive
and more than the voices I hear.

Passing the home of an elderly widow,
the lighting seems diminished
coming only from a back room,
and I sense a pervasive gray silence,
but hesitate to ring the door bell
the evening hour late.

There are homes that are welcoming,
others are houses with little warmth,
and subtle clues I've found,
sometimes greetings not returned,
never time for friendly exchange.

I recall evenings spent on porches
which neighbors' visits enlivened,
and we were summer children chasing fireflies.
When I return home from walking
past vacant porches of empty chairs,
I will sit in my old porch rocker,
and what is familiar will engage me
while I think about the walk tonight.

THESE HANDS

My hands held the tender beginnings of spring, vulnerable within uncertain tomorrows.

My hands became like the green leaves of summer, vibrant with pulsing veins, thriving in work's warmth.

My hands aged to discovered beauties of autumn, patience enfolding, holding memories never old.

My hands becoming like the cold of a winter night losing their warmth in forgotten rooms.

A ROAD THROUGH MAPLES

We never called it a street, rather a road,
some saying it was an avenue
crediting the lovely maples that lined its length.

Calling it so didn't reward the name to maps,
and now with gaps in trees from age and storm,
it can be held to question, sounding too pretentious.

Barely wide enough for two cars to meet and pass,
no spacious sidewalks adorning its narrow width,
nor stately mansions that overlooked.

It was simply our path to town,
a paved over wagon trail become a road,
passing through a tunnel of maples.

AN INNER VOICE

Deep within my most private defining,
in a site not found by probing scan
dancing into fathomless spaces.

Conflicting good intentions against wrong intent,
floating in and out of measured awareness,
zephyr-like, but bold enough to fracture doors,
or could it be the Paraclete knocking.

Always near, too near at times for comfort,
struggling with self upon the choosing,
challenging me with its intrepid presence,
conscience not sleeping, seems to know.

A LEAF FALLS NEAR

Watching a leaf in gentle free fall,
picking it up to admire design,
I learn on which tree it thrived,
sought the gift to be the wind.

I study veins etched on fading form,
threads for living to parent tree,
months of industry through summer green
ending on briefness of autumn sun.

Destiny's bequest to once be golden
before loss of anchor to that which lasts,
falling to earth on this windless day,
I think at once how lovely, how sad.

HERE IN TIME

Time disconnects best intentions,
where we stand together today.
Tomorrow will find others here,
or perhaps only you or me.

That is painful to consider,
for here should be ours forever.
Into this chosen place we came
to lose all sense of time passing.

I grieve the reason for leaving,
knowing that neither you nor I
nor place will be the same again,
the relentless hours hurry on.

A LONELY AGING DAY

Where I live has become a place of unknown faces,
and it seems to have happened overnight.
I'm glad for the few old neighbors that remain,
for Sam the cat that likes to sit atop my gate post,
and the nearby deli where I'm known.

When I look for familiar faces on my walks,
or when shopping in the big box stores,
I'm bewildered at how few people I recognize.
There was a man the other day I thought I knew,
I called him Bob, but he was Frank from Charlotte,
and I wonder if everyone has had a face lift.

My barber closed his shop, health bad,
Mr. B's hardware store vacant since he died,
and I've spent the morning wondering
where are those who were always near.

I read the other day that the voyager space ship
is eleven billion miles from earth
racing through unfamiliar interstellar space....

After breakfast I'll do some shopping
with no expectation of anyone greeting me,
although I would be glad to talk to Frank.
I'll buy another bird feeder, some seeds,
hoping to attract new visitors seeking a friend,
and welcome home those that know me.

OUR NEIGHBORS WERE FRIENDS
In Memory of the Dr. W.H. Grubb Family

Hurting deeply, but a trip I needed to make,
my dear friend would not notice,
his absence the reason for being there.
I told myself it was about family memories,
and for the widow and son, supporting presence.

It was also about fathers, mothers and sons,
years of being best neighbors, good friends.
Now two generations of mentors had passed,
no longer that same reassurance always known,
an unquestioning confidence held between families.

I miss the familiar voices, remembering laughter,
the same warm smiles at greetings and leavings,
comfort found in memories of time shared,
glad of never an awkward moment remembered,
nor need to speak of love found in friendship.

RHYTHMS OF ROCKING

This rocking chair gathers memories,
companion to previous and present musing,
bringing me in touch with a dormant past,
and when I am here, moments stretch on,
the chair an impromptu time machine.

Made for rocking, just sitting negates effect,
the gentle to and fro moves the unexpected
bringing whispers out of deepest realms,
secured places just beyond dreaming,
knowing, but needing channels to be known.
.
It rocks me through enchantment's resonance,
lost rhythms misplaced from a full life,
then endowing respect upon a rekindled time
continues rocking after my leaving,
a sense of presence remaining still.

LEAVES THAT REMAIN

Night winds had shaken our sleeping,
the November morning arriving early
finding downed limbs scattered about.
Looking at the wounded trees,
I am relieved they remain standing
while swept clean of weakest wood.

Still attached on denuded limbs
a few leaves remain, brown and wrinkled,
having lost their colors in late October,
and I wonder what anchors them
when most were lost to the wind.

They remind me of what clings tightly,
marks upon our heart's tolling,
defining us, abiding deep within,
displayed outwardly in what we do,
colored still in others' eyes beholding,
bright or faded in the light.

A WHISPER WOULD SUFFICE

How vast and silent the mystery,
as contemplating the sky tonight
full of star lights and a crescent moon,
I wonder of limits, if any to space.

Thinking of this passing moment's brevity,
I listen for sound from the quietude
arriving from the anywhere of beyond,
reaching my hearing, soft voices or vibrant strings.

I would not regret drumming or dissonance,
even a whisper would suffice, but only if I can share.
It would be too painful if it were mine alone to bear.

DRAWN BY LIGHT

When night reaches its darkest hour
I seek a reminder of the living sun,
a loss too complete, and missing its presence,
needing guidance, I am drawn to other sources,
as that which brings light offers hope.

The lights of my remembered home
provided paths for me out of dark times,
whether my return from travels near or far,
and I recall a familiar wrapping warmth
when finding known windows illumined.

Evening falls on this night of my walking,
home lights behind me quietly waiting,
and they will be there to guide my return,
soundlessly drawing, as beacon beams
to wings of moths-they will take me home.

NEVER TO CATCH A BUTTERFLY

I will not again hold a butterfly,
better a bird's lost, forgotten feather,
a rosebud sweet with morning dew.

To touch a lovely creature so soft,
that was all I intended,
catching, releasing from young hands;
then witness to a wounded flight
nearly more than I could bear.

Desperate, I helped it catch a gentle breeze
the flight once more brief and erratic,
clumsily falling, fanning one wing,
the other unable to lift the beauty.

Remembering such a thing
now past forty years,
I relive that pain once again
watching a monarch dancing on air.

TENTATIVE PRESENCE

I visit this narrow, confining space,
wishing some air were moving,
sunlight reaching within,
thinking it would be helpful
with fragrances of spring.

It seems hopelessly depressing,
a feeling of gray finality,
the bed holding a shell,
a loved one unknowing,
only hours before final grieving
when breath will be gone,
life leaving on a sigh.

From the room I will run,
wanting to know her spirit
soaring into the heavens,
and this dearly beloved
gifted to feel the breeze
lifting the sweetness of spring,
warmth of the May sun,
and she smiling broadly again.

FLEETING MEMORY

Glimpsing faces, names once known,
recalling voices etched in mind,
and I am conflicted of place and time,
one remaining, the other forever lost,
one to which I am irrevocably grounded,
the other years beyond all I loved.

Occasions of touching buried deeply
when warmth flowed freely between us,
and reaching to remember just as it was,
failing painfully, those moments gone,
and I fear becoming older than dreams allow,
hopes faltering in the fading light.

BELLA

If you read depth of affection in eyes,
I know her heart beats with love,
and it pains us that it is only for a little longer.
We feel grief she doesn't know, trying not to show,
only speaking of more shared happy days.

The attention she receives is returned
with trust and positive outlook,
even as the days of her life grow short.
She is old, but doesn't know what that means,
not well, but looks forward to a better tomorrow.

Today, we will lie in the warmth of the sun,
enjoy her favorite foods as she wishes,
hours of gentle petting, words of praise,
and at night she will again lead us to bed,
where she will sleep in the bliss of unknowing,
oblivious to the sadness welling in our eyes.

AGING THRESHERS

I found him sitting in the sun
on a day too hot for being there,
shirt cuffs and collar buttoned,
as I remembered for threshing.

Those days are now memories.
The combine changed the future,
and he wouldn't do that work
unless he was young again.

He said what he misses most
are the gathered neighbors,
work shared by lifelong friends
who tended the harvest season.

Missing the sweetness of the grain,
the intimacy of labor,
he remembers the chaff and dust,
how good the taste of spring water.

Not the same, never will be,
dust covered in the gray barn
the silent thresher rusting,
man and machine long waiting.

FALLEN WINDMILL

I look at the old windmill, scattered and rusting,
blades impotent, bent and broken on the ground
within the spaces of an ageless locust grove,
above which for many years they turned proudly
round.

A life-giving relic of an earlier time's need
nearly forgotten, with grain fields no longer here,
memories of horse drawn plows and harrows,
and where house and barn, a windmill near.

The power was captured on prevailing winds
turning these gray blades that towered high,
driving the caught energy to the gears below,
drawing upon any movement within the sky.

A common presence on our valley farms
when power needs were of daily concern,
with today's demand exceeding supply,
it may be time for the windmill to return.

TOASTING THE YEARS

We raised our glasses, searching faces,
and I can't remember if she looked older,
the lavender fragrance on her neck
near enough to touch, carefully avoiding.

Someone talked too long, not eloquent,
a failed attempt to be humorous,
his words had a dampening effect.
Another voice timidly said "No."
I looked around to see who,
and couldn't recall the name.

We won't do this next year, not all of us,
the same stories of overblown whatever,
and it has become tiresome.
My hearth and tea have more appeal,
a lavender candle better memories.

GRAY BEGINNING

The day's beginning lies hidden,
this gray room denied morning's sun,
and my hour of waking held hostage
shrouded in a blanket of fog,
closeting time and place.

Surroundings are directionless,
and I feel disconnected, forgotten.
Struggling how or why to begin,
I think beyond staring windows
where others wake in depression's plague.

I will myself not to be found sleeping,
and that enough to prod my rising.
To dispel the gray of some darker view,
I journey through the damp pale light
to unlock doors long in waiting.

AGING PETS

They are so like us as they grow old,
aging dogs and cats remind me of that,
sleeping more, moving slower, graying.
Their aches and pains, decreased senses,
some body system beginning to fail,
and they look for understanding, our patience.

They are vulnerable in their later years,
and blessed when they have caring owners.
As the aging pet's health seriously declines
their families begin to have quiet discussions,
about quality of life, costs meeting needs,
and I am asked to be an arbiter at times
helping them with making a decision.

I feel first and foremost the pet's advocate,
and when I see an aging patient in decline,
I want to find reasons to say, "It's not time."

It's difficult to overlook the positive,
a wagging tail, laughing face, hand kissing,
or in soft purring, still offered, all so adorable
when just a puppy, a kitten with so much future.

Life is a precious gift, to each once given,
and I take caution about premature closure,
considering the narrowed options,
make the best effort to be wise and fair.

DISCOVERY AT CREEK'S EDGE

I walk beside a pasture creek
staring its green mossy edges,
for some measure eyes turned earthward
where sunlight and circumstance meet.
An object, embedded in earth,
draws me near for a better look.

Finding a cutting edge rock nearby,
left when paths of waters turned,
I dig, unearthing a small skull,
intact with jaw bones and teeth,
perfectly designed to meet hunger's needs.

I consider the life this skull contained,
thoughts and fears encased therein,
hands holding once flesh covered bones,
that wore embellishing smile or frown
when blood ran warm through pulsing veins.

Considering defining size and shape,
I decide a fox, perhaps a wild dog,
knowing days of running in spirit free,
coming for rest, to drink at waters' edge,
never thoughts of life ever ending,
a blessing that simple creatures own.

I choose a green burial in answers' absence,
then placing rocks to securely cover,
hoping the integrity of a previous life
now runs and plays beneath a distant sun,
where flesh does not age or abandon bone.

NEGLECTED TOO LONG

It was a warped piece of plywood,
but it would have to do for now.
He had an aversion to ceiling wet spots,
more even than rain puddles on the floor.

They could be mopped, the stains above remained,
similar to other problems on his mind.
Lately, a loss of both sleep and energy,
and his mirror reflected a change,
the stains reminding him of that and more.

The storm last night found the neglected roof,
damage so bad, the ceiling would need replacing.
His doctor told him similar last week,
about living on borrowed time.
He thought his house was like him,
a casual observer would not see the tell-tale lines.
From a distance everything looked perfectly benign.

A RECLUSE STILL

She accepted our invitation for dinner,
a chance encounter prompting us,
and perhaps wanting to include her
more our wish that she would enjoy,
than hers finding comfort in accepting.
Surprising us, no excuses today,
a somewhat nervous smile worn,
to my "we'll pick you up at seven."
A nod of the head, byes until then.

A heavy downpour of rain
beginning at six, no letup in sight,
and the phone rang.
The voice on the other end,
sounding somewhat relieved,
declining to go out in the rain;
the excuse could be legitimate,
but her time of being a recluse
would not be broken tonight,
our efforts again finding failure,
and two years seems too long to grieve.

HERE THEY REST

Gray stones
north wind
rows of sameness
riding the hill,
not a word heard
nor laughter,
leafless trees
silently brooding,

colors gone
wilted flowers
against stones
I touch,

remembering embraces
eyes that smiled,
my mind searching
lost sharing,
staring the ground
deeply resting
beneath
names and dates,

rain slanting
wind cutting
tasting tears,
I hear my voice....

APPARITION

A fleeting presence
brushes my shoulder
willowy, floating,
pausing this gray day.

I turn quickly
feeling more than knowing,
desperate to find,
see such shadowy form.

I am left questioning
upon a spirit's journey,
briefly near,
eluding me.

My mind turning
chills the falling rain,
pulse quickening,
steps hastening.

Never in the sunlight
can you find a demon,
while the lingering one
brings intent, good or evil.

ELDERLY LADY WALKING

I see her walking with hesitant steps,
at her age not surprising, even expected,
but I find purpose in the set of her chin.
Elderly, rail thin and appearing frail,
and I think of wire like tendons connecting,
her figure again pre-adolescent.

She takes a walk daily by our house,
then turns back at the corner
her eyes looking down as she steps,
today stopping at a rain puddle's edge
presumably thinking what to do,
the shower done, the sun breaking through.

Something about her demeanor intrigues me,
watching as she considers alternatives
if indeed that is what she is doing,
and I think her best choice is to detour,
there is ample drier space to walk around,
surely that is what she will do.

After pausing, she steps forward
into the large rain puddle and stops,
lifts one foot and splashes it down,
then the other foot splashing next,
playfully repeating several times more,
and I fear she will lose her balance.

She looks around with a shy smile,
and I wonder if she knows I'm watching,
then seems to gather purpose once again
resuming her walk not as before,
but with quickened pace, more youthful,
not watching steps, looking up for a rainbow.

LOVE'S DISCOVERY

I have lived a lifetime
to reach peace in the twilight,
a willingness for eternity beyond,
discovering without doubting,
only love will free my spirit,
only love will find the light.

THE WALK OF MY LIFE

I hope that when I step into Heaven,
there to greet me are all the dogs I've loved,
friends to one another, embracing endless youth,
anxious to take me on the walk of my life.

I dream that path leads on forever through verdant fields,
with daffodils blooming beside musical creeks,
pausing there to take my fill of the pure sweet water.

Refreshed, they will guide me on to a vast hardwood forest,
where the trees one by one will step out to greet us,
becoming all the people that I have loved,
joining us in a timeless journey of promised gifts,
a walk of awareness in the presence of God.

GIFTED BY GENES

Physically I am not burdened by much,
some would say blessed by genes,
and that may be true reading these markers,
for I come to this final resting place,
at my best preferring a monologue,
surrounded by buried voices sleeping,
and ears that cannot hear the birds sing.

There is a feeling of reverence abounding,
and I remain careful in choosing words,
still uncertain, sometimes believing,
a presence hovering, nearly to speak.
My life is like theirs, and different too,
easier in this day and time to know.

My walking not behind the plow,
lifting hay in my youth, not a lifetime,
their reading had been by oil lamp.
They drank their fill of sweet spring water,
ate vegetables fertilized by cattle waste,
at night slept deeply from labors of farm.

I walk the trails and roadways,
lift and push the metal machines,
reading by lights from energy in wires,
drink filtered water that has no taste,
chemicals in vegetables not what I need,
and fall asleep when my mind tires.

I see my genes in family portraits
and sense them in the rhythm of living,
believing they still hold the spark of giving,
trusting in that to visit here and leave.

EPILOGUE

THE CANDLE

A candle in my window
to spread hope into the night,
for someone lost or hurting
may it be a guiding light.

A gift upon the dark
for others passing near,
never should a stranger
not find a welcome here.